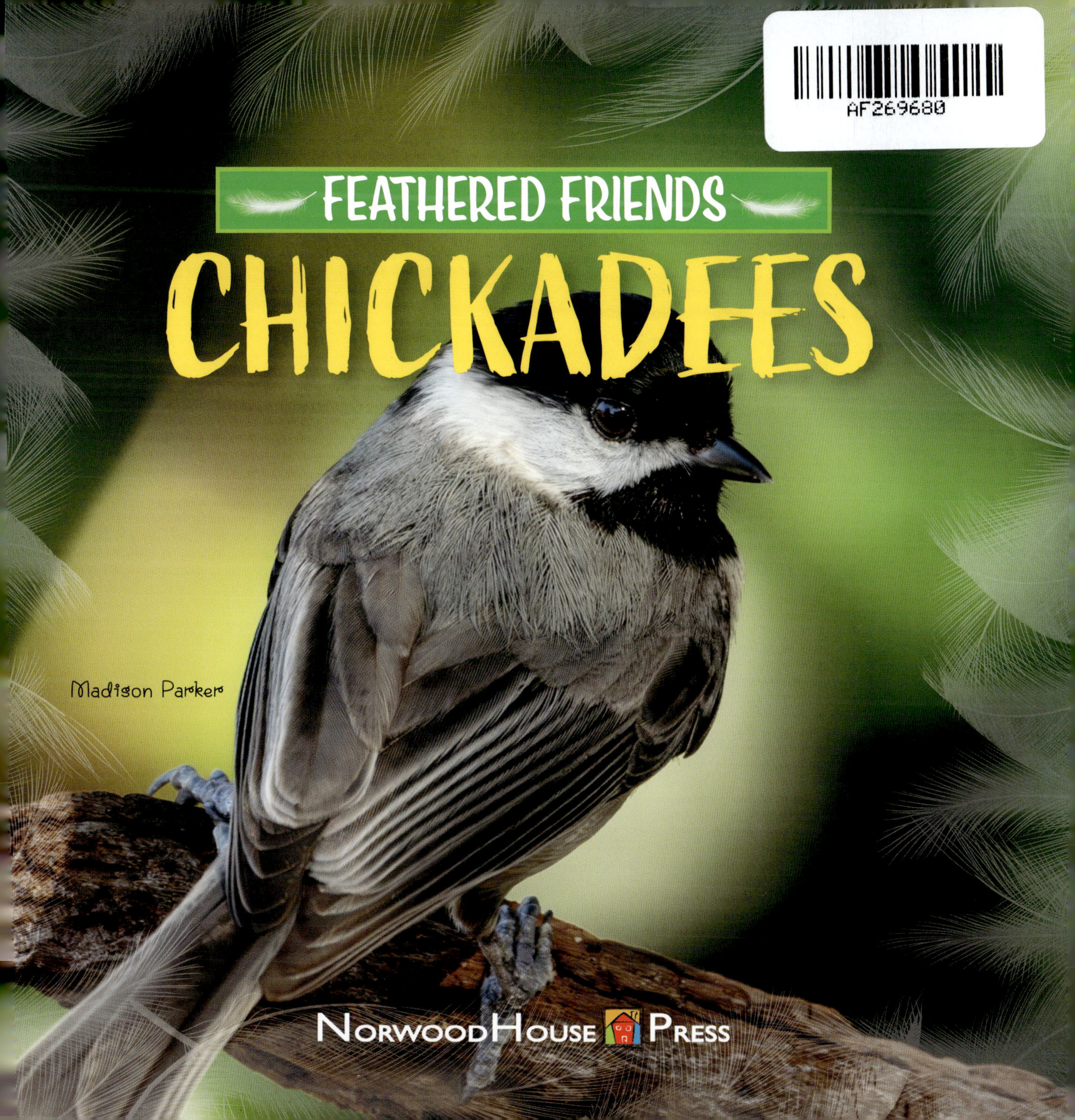

FEATHERED FRIENDS
CHICKADEES
Madison Parker
NORWOOD HOUSE PRESS

Library of Congress Cataloging-in-Publication Data:

Names: Parker, Madison.
Title: Chickadees / Madison Parker.
Description: Buffalo, NY : Norwood House Press, 2025. | Series: Feathered friends | Includes glossary and index.
Identifiers: ISBN 9781684502929 (pbk.) | ISBN 9781684502936 (library bound) | ISBN 9781684502943 (ebook)
Subjects: LCSH: Chickadees--Juvenile literature.
Classification: LCC QL696.P2615 P375 2025 | DDC 598.8'24--dc23

Published in 2025 by
Norwood House Press
2544 Clinton Street
Buffalo, NY 14224

Copyright © 2025 Norwood House Press
Designer: Ocean Books
Editor: Kim Thompson

Photo credits: Cover, p. 1 Gordon Magee/Shutterstock.com; p. 5 Christopher T Photography/Shutterstock.com; p. 6 rck_953 6/Shutterstock.com; p. 7 Christopher O'Donnell/Shutterstock.com; p. 9 Paul Reeves Photography/Shutterstock.com; p. 11 Rejean Aline Bedard/Shutterstock.com; p. 13 Nitr/Shutterstock.com; p. 15 Susan Kehoe/Shutterstock.com; p. 17 Jepp Caverly/Shutterstock.com; p. 18 Bachkova Natalia/Shutterstock.com; p. 21 Marv Vandehey/Shutterstock.com

CPSIA compliance information: Batch #CW25NHP: For further information contact Norwood House Press at 1-800-237-9932.

TABLE OF CONTENTS

What Do Chickadees Look Like?

Chickadees are our feathered friends. They are small, **puffy** birds. They have big round heads with tiny bodies.

5

Chickadee feathers are mostly gray and white. However, chickadees have **distinctive** black caps on their heads. They have black bibs under their short, stubby **beaks**.

A chickadee's long, narrow tail helps it balance.

Where Do Chickadees Live?

Chickadees live in the United States, Canada, and Mexico. They stay in one place all year.

They make nests in holes in trees. The nests are lined with **moss** and animal fur to keep eggs warm.

How Do Chickadees Grow Up?

Chickadee eggs are white with spots. Babies **hatch** in two weeks. They learn to fly in three weeks.

What Do Chickadees Eat?

Chickadees love to eat insects and spiders. They find bugs on leaves and branches.

They also eat seeds
and berries. Sometimes,
they visit bird feeders for
sunflower seeds.

To get ready for winter, chickadees hide food under tree bark or in leaves. This helps them have something to eat when there are not many bugs.

What Sounds Do Chickadees Make?

Chickadees are known for their **cheerful** calls. Their most famous sound is the "chick-a-dee-dee-dee" call.

They use this call to talk to each other. It helps them stay together when they are flying or searching for food.

When they feel safe, chickadees sing a sweet song. It sounds like "fee-bee" or "fee-bee-bee."

When **threatened**, chickadees add more "dee" sounds to their calls. This warns other chickadees to be careful.

What Funny Things Can Chickadees Do?

Chickadees like to hang upside down on branches. They do this to find tiny bugs to eat. It looks like they are little **acrobats**!

GLOSSARY

acrobats (AK-ruh-bats): skilled performers of gymnastic feats, especially while suspended in the air

beaks (beeks): horny, pointed jaws on birds; bird bills

cheerful (CHEER-fuhl): full of happiness

distinctive (di-STINGK-tiv): having a special quality or style that makes something different from others

hatch (hach): to break out of an egg to be born

moss (maws): a small, fuzzy, green plant that grows on damp soil, rocks, and tree trunks

puffy (PUH-fee): fat and round; plump

threatened (THRE-tuhnd): in danger of being harmed

THINKING QUESTIONS

1. What does a chickadee look like?

2. What is special about the sounds a chickadee makes?

3. How does a chickadee show it is smart?

4. What do chickadees eat?

5. Why do you think a chickadee is a feathered friend?

ABOUT THE AUTHOR

Madison Parker spent her childhood in the city of Chicago, Illinois. A farm girl at heart, today she lives in Wisconsin with her husband and four children on a small farm with cows, goats, chickens, and two miniature horses named Harley and David. Her favorite dessert is vanilla frozen custard with rainbow sprinkles, even in the winter.